MAKING MUSIC

Written by
Bernadette Parkhurst-Smith

THE SCIENCE OF STRING INSTRUMENTS

KidHaven PUBLISHING

Published in 2027 by
KidHaven Publishing, an Imprint of Greenhaven Publishing, LLC
2544 Clinton St., Buffalo, NY 14224

Written by: Bernadette Parkhurst-Smith
Edited by: Rebecca Phillips-Bartlett
Designed by: Ker Ker Lee

Cataloging-in-Publication Data
Names: Parkhurst-Smith, Bernadette.
Title: The science of string instruments / Bernadette Parkhurst-Smith.
Description: Buffalo, NY : KidHaven Publishing, 2027. | Series: Making music | Includes glossary and index.
Identifiers: ISBN 9781534570221 (pbk.) | ISBN 9781534570238 (library bound) | ISBN 9781534570245 (ebook)
Subjects: LCSH: Stringed instruments--Juvenile literature.
Classification: LCC ML750.P375 2027 | DDC 787.19--dc23

Printed in China

CPSIA compliance information: Batch #QS27KH: For further information contact Greenhaven Publishing LLC at 1-844-317-7404.

Please visit our website, www.greenhavenpublishing.com. For a free color catalog of all our high-quality books, call toll free 1-844-317-7404 or fax 1-844-317-7405.

Find us on

Photo Credits – Images courtesy of Shutterstock.com, unless otherwise stated.

Cover & Recurring – RidiUmbrella, SeventyFou, SeventyFour. 2–3 – Stokkete. 4–5 – vectorfusionart, MakeStory Studio. 6–7 – sirtravelalot, Joshua David Treisner. 8–9 – Tatevosian Yana, photosounds. 10–11 – Chaiya Sakc, OlhaTsiplyar. 12–13 – Ann Rodchua, eakasarn. 14–15 – Malikova Nina, MR.Yanukit. 16–17 – Roman Zaiets, Nadezda Murmakova. 18–19 – KaveeshaVisions, Odessa25. 20–21 – Bangkok Click Studio, Media_Photos. 22–23 – AlexanderSteve80, Ground Picture, Tiger Images, Cabeca de Marmore, Tony Stock, Guztsudio

CONTENTS

Words that look like <u>this</u> can be found in the glossary on page 24.

THE SCIENCE OF SOUNDS

We live in a loud world, full of lots of sounds. Musical instruments make beautiful sounds. Is it just luck that instruments sound good? Of course not! It is science!

Let's learn about what happens when we play musical instruments.

This book is all about string instruments. These instruments all have strings that have been tightly stretched. A sound is made by strumming, plucking, bowing, or hitting the strings.

This is a string quartet, which is a group of four people playing string instruments.

SOUND BASICS

A sound is a vibration. A vibration is when something quickly moves backward and forward. Some vibrations travel through the air and into the ear. The ear feels those vibrations and hears a sound.

Vibrations travel through air like a wave. This is called a sound wave.

For string instruments, the vibration is made by the string. When a string vibrates, it vibrates the air around it. This creates a sound wave. The musical sound that is made is called a note.

HARP

A harp has lots of strings. Each string makes a note with a different pitch. The pitch of a note can be high and squeaky, low and deep, or somewhere in between.

The string vibrates when you pluck it with your finger.

Thinner, shorter strings make the air vibrate more quickly, which makes notes with a higher pitch. Thicker, longer strings make the air vibrate more slowly, which makes notes with a lower pitch.

Most harps have between 22 and 47 strings.

GUITAR

A guitar normally has six strings. Each string is a different thickness. You can change the pitch by holding down a string on the fingerboard. The fingerboard is marked with metal bars called frets.

Putting your fingers at different frets makes different notes. Holding down the string means the bit of string that will vibrate is shorter. This makes a higher-pitched note.

You can pluck one string at a time or strum them all at once.

VIOLIN

A violin has four strings. Unlike a guitar, it does not have frets. You have to know exactly where to hold your finger down to make the right note.

Violins are usually played by dragging a bow across the strings.

Like most string instruments, the violin's wooden body is <u>hollow</u>. This makes the sound louder because the string also vibrates all the air inside the instrument. The sound comes out of sound holes.

The sound holes on a violin are also called f-holes.

CELLO

A cello has four strings. It is much bigger than a violin with longer, thicker strings. This means it makes lower notes. The strings are either plucked or played with a bow.

Cellos have an endpin, or spike, which rests on the ground.

To make louder sounds, you can drag the bow across the strings with more force. This will make bigger vibrations in the strings and air, which means a louder sound.

The sound is made louder with help from the hollow body and sound holes.

BANJO

A banjo usually has four or five strings. It does not have a sound hole. Instead, it has a head. This is a piece of stretched material that is like the top of a drum.

Like other instruments, the banjo's strings are stretched tightly. They can be made tighter by turning the tuning pegs. Tighter strings make higher notes. Looser strings make lower notes.

SITAR

The sitar is from India. It has a hollow body, a long hollow neck, and movable frets. Many sitars have 18 to 21 strings. On the sitar, different strings have different jobs.

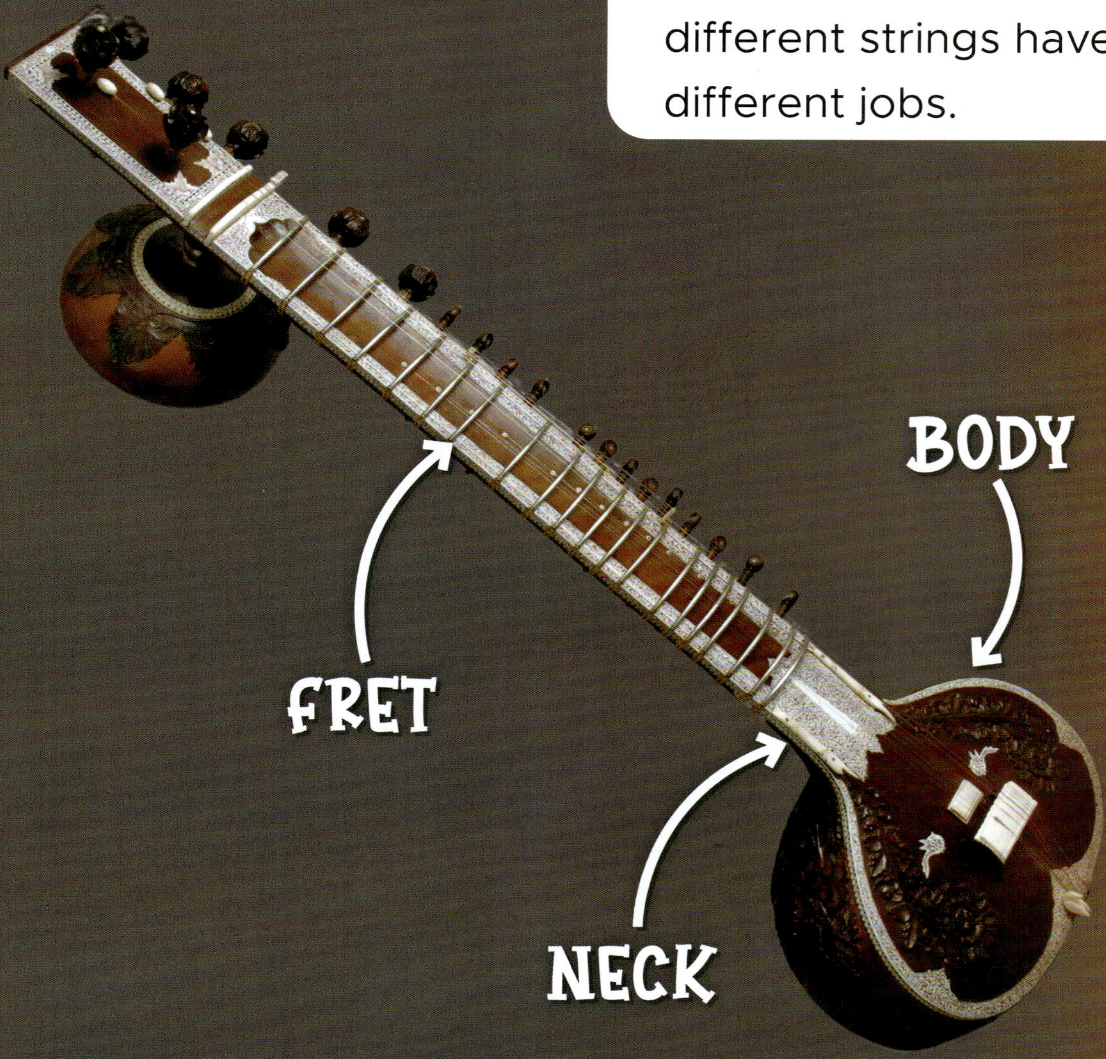

The main strings are plucked. Other strings are used for rhythm. When the main strings are plucked, some strings vibrate without being touched. These strings are free to ring, which makes a nonstop sound.

BASS GUITAR

A bass guitar usually has four strings. The metal strings are very thick, which means it can play very low notes. The body is made of wood, but it is not hollow.

The material of the string changes the tone of the instrument.

Bass guitars use amps to make the sounds louder. Vibrations from the strings travel into pickups, down a wire, and to the amp. Amps then use electricity to make a loud sound.

PIANO

A piano might not look like a string instrument, but inside it can have around 230 strings. When you press a key, a hammer hits a string to make it vibrate.

You now know the science of string instruments, but what about playing an instrument yourself? Choose your favorite, and soon you will be making music!

You could even make your own string instrument using everyday objects!

GLOSSARY

bowing in music, dragging a bow across a string to make a musical sound on a string instrument

fingerboard the part of an instrument underneath the strings where the player places their fingers to hold down the strings and make different notes

force a push or pull on an object

hollow not full, has air or empty space inside

material what something is made of

plucking in music, pulling a string lightly with the finger to make a sound

rhythm a pattern of sounds usually made by a percussion instrument that follows the beat of the music

strumming dragging the tips of the fingers across the strings to make musical sounds

tone the characteristics of a musical sound that make it sound different from others

INDEX